TWO AS ONE

CONNECTING **DAILY** WITH
CHRIST AND YOUR SPOUSE

A 30-Day Devotional by
RYAN & SELENA FREDERICK

AN [INSTAVOTIONAL]™

TWO AS ONE

CONNECTING DAILY WITH CHRIST AND YOUR SPOUSE

Published by Cormens Press
a division of Vilicus Holdings Ltd.

ISBN-13: 978-0-9974713-0-4 (pbk. bw.)

Printing/manufacturing information for this book may be found on the last page.

This book is dedicated

to the countless couples who have

poured into us over the years.

You know who you are.

Thank you for encouraging, equipping,

and helping us in our journey.

CONTENTS

CONTENTS

A NOTE FROM THE AUTHORS

Hello, we're Ryan & Selena Frederick, co-authors of FierceMarriage.com. We've been married since 2003 and since our wedding day we've experienced plenty of ups and downs. We don't know everything, but we promise to share what we do know honestly and transparently.

We pray that this book strengthens your marriage by bringing you closer to Jesus and each other. We also hope it helps you develop a consistent devotional habit as a couple.

Find all joy and meaning in Christ, and may his hope, love, and peace overwhelm you as you're transformed into the spouse he's calling you to be. Thank you for reading!

Stay fierce,

Ryan & Selena Frederick

OUR PRAYER FOR YOU

Father,

Thank you for your word and for helping us understand it. We ask that you use this resource to strengthen couples for their joy and your ultimate glory. Fortify marriages and embolden spouses to love each other more radically, faithfully, and purposefully than ever before.

Please fill each reader with inexplicable hope and a sweet conviction to change in areas where it's needed most. Mould each man or woman who turns these pages into the spouse you're calling them to be. Change hearts, renew minds, and help them bear fruit in their marriage that glorifies you.

More than anything, we want—*we need*—more of you. Draw us near. You're the ultimate prize, and may knowing you more closely be our life's grandest pursuit.

In Jesus' name, amen.

GETTING THE MOST FROM THIS RESOURCE

This devotional is designed to be easily read and practically applied. It's not exhaustive on any one topic, and that's intentional. We aim to help you to connect with each other and establish a habit of studying the Bible regularly as a couple. Whether you're newly married or celebrating decades together, you're sure to find something on each page to get you thinking.

We encourage you to use *Two as One* as a **supplement** to your individual devotional time; there is simply no replacement for reading Scripture in depth and at length.

EACH DAY INCLUDES FOUR SECTIONS

See: An image is provided with an inspirational or thought-provoking quote. This is the day's conversation kick-off point, so take time to read and think about its meaning.

Read: We've provided commentaries and verses for each day. While the passage *is* provided, we encourage you to open your Bible and **read the surrounding context**. Let God's word read you!

Reflect & apply: Answer the discussion questions together, honestly and thoughtfully.

Pray: Each day concludes with a blank page for you each to write a short prayer. Think of it as a combined prayer journal where you solidify what God is teaching you that day. Use it!

always remember...

[JESUS
CHANGES
EVERYTHING.]

not you.

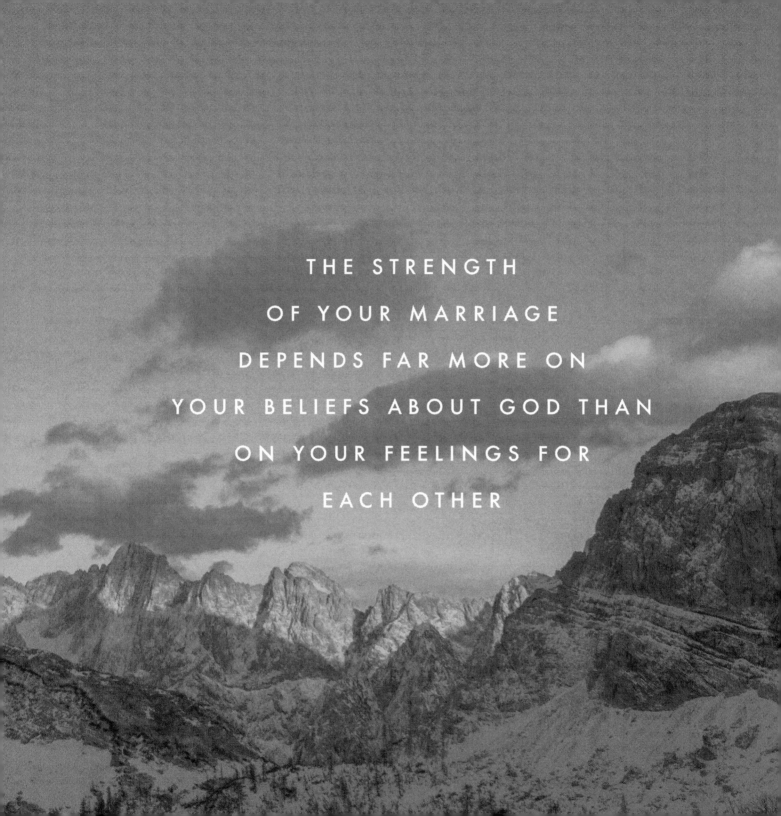

THE STRENGTH
OF YOUR MARRIAGE
DEPENDS FAR MORE ON
YOUR BELIEFS ABOUT GOD THAN
ON YOUR FEELINGS FOR
EACH OTHER

DAY 1: ROCKS, ROCKETS, & THE GRAVITY OF BELIEF

Your beliefs about God have an immeasurable impact on your marriage. They affect how you view each other, yourself, and the purpose of your union. If you try to change behavior without tackling underlying beliefs, the changes will rarely stick. That's because every perspective, expectation, and behavior stems from belief. As Paul writes, beliefs only change by renewing your mind:

"Do not be conformed to this world, but be transformed by the renewal of your mind, that by testing you may discern what is the will of God, what is good and acceptable and perfect." (Romans 12:2)

Unless your belief is in Christ, your mind remains unchanged and conformed to this world.

Think of belief as gravity and your behavior as a one pound rock. You're tasked with keeping the rock in the air as long as possible. You toss it up but it always falls back to the ground. You may build a contraption to launch it five miles into the sky. You might even engineer some wings and a rocket to make it fly. With a lot of work, scheming, and fuel, you may be able to keep it up for an hour or two. In **all** cases, the rock will always fall to the ground. What if your life depended on keeping this rock in the air forever? What if the rock weighed 5 lbs? 20 lbs? 1000 lbs? The heavier the rock, the lower your chances for success. Unless... *what if you reversed the law of gravity?* Then everything would change.

Belief in Jesus changes everything. Fix your eyes on him; he'll renew your mind and change your heart.

DISCUSSION QUESTIONS

Can you think of a few areas where your beliefs have affected your behavior toward your spouse?

(Think: how do you usually react to various situations and why?)

Have you and your spouse firmly established your beliefs in Christ? How so?

Do you have your family beliefs written down anywhere?

HIS PRAYER

The LAST 2 years of HURT

HER PRAYER

SO THEY ARE NO LONGER
TWO BUT ONE FLESH.
WHAT THEREFORE GOD
HAS JOINED TOGETHER
LET MAN NOT SEPARATE.

Matthew 19:6

DAY 2: NO LONGER TWO

When you stood together at the altar and said "I do", you became one flesh. You each promised to treat your spouse's well being as if it were your own. In fact, most vows include promises to seek the other's good *before* your own and journey through life in lock-step—inseparable and unified.

"So they are no longer two but one flesh. What therefore God has joined together, let not man separate." (Matthew 19:6)

Jesus said those words right after the Pharisees asked him why Moses would allow divorce. Divorce was permitted because of the hardness of heart and divorce culture that permeated Israel. It was never the norm, but rather a concession made for those whose hearts were too far gone.

Divorce is never God's best. You will face frequent challenges in your marriage, but your heart must remain soft. The alternative (a hardened heart) will devastate your life and your relationship. Hardness of heart inhibits oneness by starving your life of repentance. Ask God to soften your hearts and keep you tender to what he is saying. In each instance, the Holy Spirit will faithfully minister to you, convict as needed, and lead you to repent.

Your heart's condition always affects your spouse; you're **one** flesh in God's eyes. Work together to keep your hearts soft by working through everything and removing divorce as an option.

DISCUSSION QUESTIONS

Are there areas of your heart that are hardening or have hardened? Where, and why?

How can you help each other keep soft hearts if/when marriage gets difficult? Be specific.

HIS PRAYER

HER PRAYER

I AM MY BELOVED'S

& MY BELOVED IS MINE

Song of Solomon 6:3

DAY 3: THE BLESSED FOUNTAIN

Many couples struggle with unity about sex and finding fulfillment in the bedroom. Marriage provides the best imaginable context for sex, and you're called to enjoy it thoroughly within its bounds. This passage uses vivid language to encourage you to take pleasure in each other sexually:

"Let your fountain be blessed, and rejoice in the wife of your youth, a lovely deer, a graceful doe. Let her breasts fill you at all times with delight; be intoxicated always in her love" (Proverbs 5:18-19)

God created sex to be magnificent in marriage! Here are three thoughts for building a healthy sex life:

1) Great sex takes time. It only gets better as your marriage matures and your bond strengthens. Every healthy married couple we've spoken to agrees. Give it time, learn, and be patient.

2) Great sex takes communication. The beauty of sex within marriage is that you can be completely confident and open with each other. Create a "safe zone" where you can express yourselves honestly and lovingly respond. Talk about your sex life: what you love, dislike, and desire to explore. Just talk.

3) Great sex takes practice. It's not about practicing "sex" as much as it is learning about your spouse. Learn each other's needs and wants through communication, then spend *lots* of time practicing!

In all things, keep your marriage bed pure: no degradation of dignity, purely selfish acts, pornography, or anything that dishonors God. As you do, you'll enjoy an intimate, vibrant, and healthy sex life!

DISCUSSION QUESTIONS

What is the purpose of sexual intimacy in your marriage? Why?

What are two tangible ways you can grow in your sex life?

HIS PRAYER

HER PRAYER

IF WE'RE TOO BUSY
FOR EACH OTHER,
WE'RE TOO BUSY.

DAY 4: BUSIER ISN'T BETTER

This is a general rule for us: if we're too busy for each other, we're too busy. If we're not careful, we can fill our lives with so many "good" things that we miss out on the most important things. Martha made that mistake when she missed out on Jesus' presence because she was too busy:

But the Lord answered her, "Martha, Martha, you are anxious and troubled about many things, but one thing is necessary. Mary has chosen the good portion, which will not be taken away from her."
(Luke 10:41-42)

Mary chose Jesus, Martha chose duty. Don't make Martha's mistake. There are many important things to spend your time on. Many are good but only a few are indispensable:

1) **Time with God.** Grow in your relationships with God. Spend time with him, read his word. Pray throughout your day and just *be* with him. He is the ultimate prize both now and forever.

2) **Time with your spouse.** Whatever you feed grows, and what you starve dies. Invest in your relationship, spend quality time together and have meaningful conversations.

3) **Time with your kids.** Spend time as a family building each other up. You'll never regret a minute spent with those God has placed in your immediate life, and the generation impact is immense.

Busier isn't better, and it takes diligence to craft an intentional schedule, but it's well worth the work.

DISCUSSION QUESTIONS

What are some areas in your life that are too busy? Think of one good thing that may not be the best choice given the priorities mentioned.

Can you adjust your schedule so it better reflects your priorities? How so? Be specific.

HIS PRAYER

HER PRAYER

THE MOST BEAUTIFUL
ASPECT OF A WOMAN
IS HER HEART FOR CHRIST

DAY 5: CREATED BEAUTIFUL

The world shows us that a woman's attractiveness comes from her clothes, makeup, and body shape. Modern culture also tells us that beauty is found in a woman's self, her confidence, or her ability to thoughtfully articulate ideas.

While those qualities of a woman can show aspects of her external and internal beauty, they're not the true **source** of it. Any beauty we see or experience in this world is a shadow of the One who created beauty itself, and a glimpse of our vast God who authored our very desire to pursue it.

"He has made everything beautiful in its time. He has also set eternity in the human heart; yet no one can fathom what God has done from beginning to end." (Ecclesiastes 3:11)

True beauty belongs to God, and you are most beautiful when you reflect glory to him most clearly.

Fierce wife, let your confidence, value, and worth come from the **only** source of all that is truly beautiful: your Creator. In him you are astoundingly beautiful.

Fierce husband, love and lead your bride in light of her intrinsic beauty in Jesus. Viewing her as a daughter of the King will forever change how you treat and value your bride.

DISCUSSION QUESTIONS

Wife, have you struggled with feeling beautiful or 'worthy of love'? In what ways?

How does understanding who you are in Christ change that? Be as specific as possible.

Husband, what are three ways you can regularly remind your wife of her beauty in Christ?

HIS PRAYER

HER PRAYER

MY SPOUSE IS A
WORTHWHILE PURSUIT

DAY 6: A WORTHWHILE PURSUIT

Your wedding day doesn't mark the end of your pursuit of each other, it's just the beginning! Pursuing your spouse means you realize that you can always love him/her more–you *want* more.

"How beautiful and pleasant you are, O loved one, with all your delights!" (Song of Solomon 7:6)

This passage shows a beautiful picture of unquenchable love. By pursuing your spouse, you're saying you can't get enough of them! You will never stop learning about them or learning the intricacies of how to love them. Here are some practical ways you can pursue each other:

1) Surprise them with a thoughtful gesture. Flowers? A spontaneous date? Do something around the house he/she wouldn't expect you to do? Unexpected intimacy? Take initiative!

2) Write a note. When was the last time you hand wrote a love letter to your spouse? Don't forget the unique power of pen and paper. Consider writing a song or a poem, just be you!

3) Express appreciation with genuine compliments. Let your words be words of pursuit. What do you love about each other? What's your favorite facial feature or personality quirk? What character traits do you admire most?

This list is just a beginning, the rest is up to you. Get creative, be yourselves, and pursue each other with everything you've got.

DISCUSSION QUESTIONS

How can you purposefully pursue each other daily? Think of at least three tangible examples.

How do you desire to be pursued? What can your spouse do to make you feel most loved?

HIS PRAYER

HER PRAYER

A MARRIAGE

BUILT ON CHRIST

IS A MARRIAGE

BUILT TO LAST

DAY 7: CHRIST IS ENOUGH

So much of daily life involves others telling us they have what we need; that somehow their product, solution, or way of thinking will finally be the thing that unlocks ultimate happiness. If we're not careful we start to believe them... even if we don't realize it at first.

Thoughts like, *"If we could just buy that house, we'd be happy"* or *"if I could only lose 20 lbs, I'd feel comfortable and confident"* flood our minds. While some desires like these are healthy, they become toxic when we make them our source of identity. Like all false idols, they will fail every single time.

The gospel points us toward the only thing worth seeking:

"But seek first the kingdom of God and his righteousness, and all these things will be added to you." (Matt 6:33)

When Jesus is the central goal of your life, you'll have the most valuable thing you could ever ask for: a loving Savior and adoption into God's family. As a byproduct, you receive more joy, hope, and wisdom than you could possibly find anywhere or in anyone else.

Seek Christ first as individuals and as a couple. Build your entire marriage on Jesus. He alone is worthy of every ounce of worship you can give... and a thousand times more!

DISCUSSION QUESTIONS

What's one area of your life where you can trust more in Christ's sufficiency as a couple? Have you unknowingly built idols and placed your hope in them?

How can you grow in your relationships with Christ alongside one another? Through reading the Bible? Prayer? Deeper involvement in your church community? Write down specific ways.

HIS PRAYER

HER PRAYER

HAPPY IS THE MAN
WHO FINDS A TRUE FRIEND,
AND FAR HAPPIER IS HE WHO
FINDS THAT THE TRUE FRIEND
IS HIS WIFE.

Frank Schubert

DAY 8: FOUNDATIONAL FRIENDSHIP

Godly friendship is endearing, honest, encouraging, challenging, and deeply committed all at the same time. The biblical model of friendship is unlike any other in history. It is *fiercely loving*. That's the type of friendship you should cultivate in your marriage. It's the kind that sharpens, honors, respects, listens, and fights on behalf of one another.

"A friend loves at all times, and a brother is born for adversity." (Proverbs 17:17)

There are too many biblical examples of friendship to summarize here, but the above verse encapsulates them well: *a friend loves at all times*. Remember your roles as friends to each other.

Spouses can grow too familiar with one another. Familiarity makes you forget common courtesies like not interrupting, listening energetically, being slow to pass judgement, and showing basic manners out of mutual respect.

Husband, treat your wife well! Open doors, give her compliments, take interest in the things that interest her. Wife, express gratitude! Love your husband in ways he'll feel most loved, and remember the influence you have on his heart by encouraging him intentionally.

By strengthening your friendship you're building your marriage and the investment is always worth it.

DISCUSSION QUESTIONS

What are three tangible ways you can be a better friend to your spouse?

What are a few activities that you can do together to intentionally build your friendship? Take time to plan at least two and write them in the space below.

HIS PRAYER

HER PRAYER

MARRIAGE IS AN
UNPARALLELED ADVENTURE

DAY 9: AN UNPARALLELED ADVENTURE

Every good adventure story has lots of excitement and plenty of peril. There are friends to be made and foes to be defeated. Similarly, marriage is a lifelong, epic adventure with your spouse. You'll have many incredible times and other moments when you feel like you're fighting for your lives.

Here's one key to every marital journey: fight side by side instead of against one another.

Some moments you may feel like you're lost the marriage "wilderness". Trust the Bible as your map and guide. In it, God promises the path to lasting victory in Christ.

Nevertheless, I am continually with you; you hold my right hand. You guide me with your counsel, and afterward you will receive me to glory. (Psalm 73:23-24)

There will be times in life and marriage when you question how your journey will end. Remember who the hero of your story is: **Jesus.** It's not you, it's not your spouse. **Just Jesus.**

Jesus is with you the entire way. He's won the fight, defeated the foe, and secured your place as God's adopted, dearly loved children. God always takes care of his children! Place your full trust in Christ, lean on him, and find rest in his promises throughout every leg of your journey together.

As you trust in Jesus through each battle, your victory is secure because your hero is sure.

DISCUSSION QUESTIONS

How can you better fight *alongside* instead of *against* each other?

How can you rely more completely on Jesus as your hero and the Bible as your map? Think of a few concrete examples.

HIS PRAYER

HER PRAYER

OUR VOWS ARE PROMISES
TO PERSEVERE THROUGH
EVERY CIRCUMSTANCE.

THEY'RE NOT PROMISES
OF PERFECTION.

DAY 10: PERSEVERANCE ≠ PERFECTION

Remember your vows? They probably included something like "*...to have and to hold, for richer and for poorer, in sickness and in health, until death do us part.*"

These are promises to endure the good times along with the bad. It's also important to remember what they're not: vows to be **perfect**. It's neither helpful nor biblical to hold yourself or your spouse to a standard of perfection. There's only one person the history of mankind who was perfect: Jesus. You aren't perfect. No one is. Here's the good news: you're clothed in Christ's perfection free of charge:

"For our sake he made him to be sin who knew no sin, so that in him we might become the righteousness of God. Working together with him, then, we appeal to you not to receive the grace of God in vain."
(2 Corinthians 5:21-6:1)

Your vows are promises to serve each other and seek the good of each other before your own. They're not promises of perfection! Christ's was the only promise of perfection and only he could fulfill it. When we understand that Christ's perfection is a gift, we're filled with gratitude and emptied of self-righteousness. This levels the playing field in a marriage between two incredibly imperfect people.

Flood your marriage with patience and forgiveness. Handle imperfections with grace, and always remember the bottom line: your perfection is a free gift, one far too expensive to purchase yourself.

DISCUSSION QUESTIONS

Have you unknowingly expected yourself or your spouse to be perfect? How can understanding the gospel change your expectations?

Read Hebrews 10:10-14. How is your positional perfection in Christ (right-standing before God) different from "being sanctified" or "being made holy"? How does this distinction affect how you should view one another in marriage?

HIS PRAYER

HER PRAYER

LOVE SAYS: I'VE SEEN
THE UGLY PARTS OF YOU
AND I'M STAYING

Matt Chandler

DAY 11: FULLY KNOWN & FULLY LOVED

An unmistakeable intimacy occurs when you're utterly exposed and *still* totally loved. Intimacy is the deepest level of "knowing", and it's what the Bible is referring to when discussing the consummation of marriage (sex) by using the verb "to know".

You're called to "know" each other on the deepest levels imaginable between two people (physical, emotional, spiritual, intellectual). It's this deep intimacy and *knowing* that makes true love possible; you can only love the parts that are made known. In light of knowing each other so intimately, you're instructed to love one another relentlessly as Christ loves the church.

"If your brother sins against you, go and tell him his fault, between you and him alone. If he listens to you, you have gained your brother." (Matthew 18:15)

That may seem like an odd verse, but it's especially relevant. Jesus is addressing the disciples after they asked "who is the greatest in the Kingdom of heaven?" In response, he discusses faith like children, temptation, lost sheep, reconciliation, and forgiveness. **It's a model of being known and loved.** Jesus calls them to have transparent faith, confront sin, seek reconciliation, repent, and forgive. This is perfect love. Aside from Christ, perfect love is impossible. His love gives you the *power to love* you desperately need to be reconciled time and time again. May your love be the kind that endures even when your spouse's *ugly* is showing. That's Christ-like love, and it is truly freeing.

DISCUSSION QUESTIONS:

How can you be more transparent with your husband/wife with the goal of total intimacy? Are you fully known by your spouse?

How can you show Christ-like love and grace to your spouse when their "ugly is showing"? What does the reconciliation process look like?

HIS PRAYER

HER PRAYER

NOTHING REPLACES
GENUINE FRIENDSHIP
BETWEEN SPOUSES

DAY 12: LAUGH, LISTEN, LOVE

Remember that you began as friends. Your earliest moments as a couple likely included plenty of conversation, laughter, and fun. Your foundation of friendship will sustain you when feelings of romance come and go. Celebrate your history together! Laugh more, encourage constantly, listen intently, and share transparently. Consider this passage:

"When the Lord restored the fortunes of Zion, we were like those who dream. Then our mouth was filled with laughter, and our tongue with shouts of joy; then they said among the nations, 'The Lord has done great things for them.' The Lord has done great things for us; we are glad." (Psalm 126:1-3)

As believers in Christ, you have cause to celebrate! You have cause to dream, laugh, shout with joy, and be glad! Why? Because the Lord has done great things. It's from that place of understanding Christ's goodness that you realize your true reason for joy–for fun. That underlying reason for your joy will drastically affect the culture of your friendship in marriage.

There are no shortcuts to building a deep friendship. It takes time, honesty, diligence in learning about one another, and celebrating the unending goodness of God in Christ. Make time to build and strengthen your friendship. Have fun and celebrate your life together! Talk and listen!

A rich, healthy friendship will increase the joy and unity in your household for years to come.

DISCUSSION QUESTIONS

What does it mean to be a *good* friend?

What are three tangible ways you can build your friendship both today and on a regular basis?

HIS PRAYER

HER PRAYER

THE HAPPINESS OF MARRIED
LIFE DEPENDS UPON MAKING
SMALL SACRIFICES WITH
READINESS & CHEERFULNESS.

John Seldon

DAY 13: THE GENEROUS MARRIAGE

Healthy marriage is not as much "give and take", but more "give and give". True, each receives from the other, but the focus of marriage must be to give generously on every level. Generosity is a huge part of marriage because giving is a natural outflow of love. God **gave** His only son in the most magnificent act of love of all time:

"For God so loved the world that he gave His only son..." (John 3:16a)

Indeed this is a familiar verse, and for good reason. It encapsulates everything God did in Christ and *why*. There is one unique aspect of John 3:16 that is often overlooked: he *gave*.

Giving is a product of love. God loved, so he *gave*. It's a natural progression. Cause and effect.

As you learn to love, you learn more about truly giving of yourself. Love gives grace, love gives effort, love gives affection, love gives time, and love gives everything it possibly can to the one loved. There is nothing perfect love won't give for its beloved. The problem is that we're not perfect, and we don't often love each other perfectly.

But God helps us along. By his grace and guidance, we learn to love more perfectly. Be generous with each other, always seek each other's good before your own, and when in doubt, *give*.

DISCUSSION QUESTIONS

What's one instance in the past when you could have been more generous with each other? Why do you think you chose not to give what they needed (time, words of encouragement, etc.)?

How can you be more generous toward each other moving forward? Be specific.

HIS PRAYER

HER PRAYER

MARRIAGE IS LIKE A HOUSE.
WHEN A LIGHT GOES OUT
YOU DON'T BUY A NEW HOUSE,
YOU REPLACE THE BULB.

DAY 14: KEEP THE HOUSE, TOSS THE BULB

We live in a "throw away" culture. If we're not careful this attitude can permeate our lives in areas that matter most, marriage included. The quote to the left (author unknown) is powerful because it reminds us that we mustn't be too quick to discard our whole marriage when parts of it simply need renewal, removal, or replacement. Otherwise, the cost is too great and the sacrifice unnecessary.

"Bad bulbs" accumulate quickly when left unattended. They gradually darken the rooms and hallways of your home as darkness creeps in where light is absent. In marriage, bad bulbs can be hurts unexpressed, forgiveness withheld, or a lack of good habits that were never established. There's great news! Christ's light pierces every dim space, and darkness never overcomes it.

"The light shines in the darkness, and the darkness has not overcome it." (John 1:5)

All areas of sin and discord–*darkness*–are rooted in an implicit disbelief in the gospel. When you hide sin or let it wreak havoc in your marriage, you set aside the goodness of Christ and what he's done to grab hold of something else. You replace his lordship with your own and craft idols, made of either pride or fear. Without the gospel, idols pile up and darkness follows. After enough rooms grow unlivable, you'll want to move out. The key to sustaining marriage is not in replacing bad bulbs with new bulbs of the same nature, it's in replacing your brokenness with Christ's completeness. Don't sell the house, keep it! Just replace bad bulbs with the only light that will never fade: Jesus.

DISCUSSION QUESTIONS

Are there any "bad bulbs" or "dark hallways" in your marriage? In other words, do you have any unresolved or hidden issues that should be brought to light?

How can you *sustainably* replace your bad bulbs with the light of Christ? What changes are needed?

HIS PRAYER

HER PRAYER

"DRAW ME AFTER YOU, LET US RUN."

Song of Solomon 1:4

DAY 15: LOST IN INTIMACY

Marriage is such a beautiful, vivid picture of unbridled passion and love. In it, both husband and wife are uniquely poised to chase after one another and find God-blessed pleasure and intimacy.

The whole text of Song of Solomon describes a mutually adoring and helplessly enamored relationship shared by a man and woman in marriage. You get a sense of just how consumed both parties are by their pursuit of each other. It is a book marked by sensual imagery and sexual intimacy. They are intoxicated by one another. This is a good design, and an unparalleled blessing from God. This one verse encapsulates the book's theme perfectly:

"Draw me after you, let us run." (Song of Solomon 1:4)

Most incredibly, the mutual pursuit and deep affections described throughout Song of Solomon are parallels to the relationship between Christ and his bride, the Church. He is deeply in love with you and has stopped at nothing—not even death—to pursue you. What a remarkable and life changing idea to grasp! And what amazing depth it adds to the meaning of your marriage!

May you and your spouse be lost in love. Pursue each other passionately and enjoy being pursued by your beloved. Even more than that, always remember how you're relentlessly pursued by the ultimate lover of your soul: Jesus.

DISCUSSION QUESTIONS

Think back to one incredible sexual experience you've shared. What made it so memorable?

HIS PRAYER

HER PRAYER

GOD ALONE
CHANGES HEARTS.
WE ARE SIMPLY
CALLED TO LOVE.

DAY 16: WORKS IN PROGRESS

Remember: God is working on your heart as much as he's working on your spouse's.

Many times, we see a character flaw in our spouse that we want to change, so we get to work trying to fix parts of them that are "broken". This materializes as nagging, complaining, and arguing about everything the other person is doing wrong.

Don't assume too much power over changing your spouse. Instead, trust God to finish the work he started. Paul wrote an incredible encouragement to believers:

"And I am sure of this, that he who began a good work in you will bring it to completion at the day of Jesus Christ." (Philippians 1:6)

God claims all responsibility for changing hearts. But too often we like to jump in and offer suggestions on what he should work on first. That's not your job! It's way above your pay grade. Sure, we can lovingly encourage each other and encourage one another toward right-living, but never from a place of self-righteousness or pride.

As a spouse, love freely; the same way Christ has loved you. Then, relax and let God do what only he can do: change hearts. It's a task He is well qualified to perform.

DISCUSSION QUESTIONS

What's one way God is currently at work in both of your hearts? How do you know he's working?

How can you pray more intentionally for each other instead of trying 'fix' flaws yourself?

HIS PRAYER

HER PRAYER

QUALITY TIME:

NO SHORTCUTS

NO SUBSTITUTES

DAY 17: NO SHORTCUTS, NO SUBSTITUTES

Every day is full distraction opportunities: phones, television, browsing the internet, work, over-committing to activities at church or with friends, the list goes on. Everything and everyone is fighting for your attention. Make building emotional intimacy in your marriage a priority. Otherwise, you risk losing closeness as you go from task to task and from one distraction to another. David understood life's brevity in this often quoted passage:

"Surely all mankind stands as a mere breath!" (Psalm 39:5b)

The big reminder here is to **not** waste time. Here are three ways to have quality time intentionally:

1) Date nights. Why not schedule standing appointments? Block out times on your calendar in advance, then honor your commitments like they're the most important meetings all week (they are).

2) Have meaningful conversations. When you're together, put distractions aside and talk about important things. Ask probing questions and go further in your conversations.

3) Get out! Sometimes a coffee or ice cream date does just the trick. Dates don't need to be expensive or elaborate to be incredible. Be intentionally spontaneous. Get out of the house as often as possible.

Here's an idea: schedule "QT" (Quality Time) blocks in your calendars and alternate who's responsible for planning them! Get creative, have fun, and make unforgettable memories.

DISCUSSION QUESTIONS

What's one distraction that consistently takes away from the quality time you spend together?

How can you make quality time a consistent priority? Start by brainstorming and planning at least two dates over the next 30 days.

HIS PRAYER

HER PRAYER

REFRAIN FROM THROWING
PAST HURTS IN YOUR SPOUSE'S FACE
DURING AN ARGUMENT.

SEEK RECONCILIATION
OVER RETALIATION

DAY 18: RECONCILIATION OVER RETALIATION

Whenever two people commit to a lifetime together, they'll inevitably argue and experience hurts. That's why it's extremely important to work together toward full reconciliation each time. You have a lifetime to get hurt, and the same lifetime to live with resentment if it's not dealt with.

The Bible's model of reconciliation is designed for resolution of conflict and restoration of relationships. You deal with the conflict to resolve the underlying issue, all with the end goal of restoring the relationship. It's not always easy, but it's always right.

"Put on then, as God's chosen ones, holy and beloved, compassionate hearts, kindness, humility, meekness, and patience, bearing with one another and, if one has a complaint against another, forgiving each other; as the Lord has forgiven you, so you also must forgive." (Colossians 3:12-13)

God doesn't set this standard for us lightly, and it's the primary reason Jesus humbled himself to death on the cross. Remember the grace you're given in Christ to be called "God's chosen ones, holy and beloved". He gave his life so you could be reconciled to him. Can you give grace too?

When you function out of fear and pride (sin) you tend to seek retaliation in order to feel better. But when you operate knowing the price Christ paid on your behalf, you're filled with gratitude, grace, the capacity to forgive, and a genuine desire for reconciliation.

DISCUSSION QUESTIONS

Can you think of an example where you tend to seek retaliation when you're hurt? Why is that your tendency?

How can you seek reconciliation when future conflicts arise? In other words, what are the "rules of engagement" for disagreements between you?

HIS PRAYER

HER PRAYER

81

NO BACKUP PLANS.

NO ESCAPE CLAUSES.

ZERO REGRETS.

DAY 19: LIVES MARKED BY PURSUIT

There's profound joy in the mutual and reckless pursuit of each other in marriage. Marriage requires a fierce tenacity that never gives up and never gives in. What does this reckless pursuit actually look like in marriage? What enables it within every complex issue and circumstance you will face?

To start, look at Christ's example. He pursues you without fail. It's his steady pursuit that drew you to him, and it's because of his love and grace alone that you're in relationship with him.

"Where shall I go from your Spirit? Or where shall I flee from your presence? If I ascend to heaven, you are there! If I make my bed in Sheol, you are there!" (Psalm 139:7-8)

The psalmist is reflecting on God's limitless pursuit of those he loves. The concept of a *pursuing love* has immense implications for your marriage.

Pursuit is active, not passive. It means to chase steadily with the goal of *capture*. This is why it's vital to keep dating each other long after you marry. When you work with the expressed intent of capturing your spouse's heart, you're in active pursuit. And more importantly, when you're having a hard time connecting, the pursuit **continues**. May you throw out any and all backup plans in your marriage. When you do, you'll enjoy the intimacy that comes only from pursuing unconditionally and being pursued exactly the same way.

DISCUSSION QUESTIONS

How can you "recklessly pursue" each other in light of God's pursuit of you?

How do you enjoy being pursued by your spouse? Be specific.

PRAY

HIS PRAYER

HER PRAYER

PRAY | PLAY | STAY

TOGETHER

DAY 20: PRAY, PLAY, STAY

Sometimes the simplest concepts cause the most powerful impact. One phrase we like to use often in our own relationship is this: *"pray, play, stay... always together"*.

Here's what we mean by each word:

Pray together: Bring your entire lives before God. Talk to him often and together. When you pray, you acknowledge your trust and faith in God. You deepen your relationship with him as your Father, Savior, and King. This will unify, strengthen, and encourage you in every way.

Play together: Be friends. Be intentional about building your relationship and enjoying each other's company. Find activities you can do together. Laugh with each other and find joy in one another. Remind yourselves of your friendship often as possible.

Stay together: When the fun moments are few and far between or times get tough, simply stick together through it. The winter will pass. There's a beautiful sense of security when you're both committed to working through anything and everything. Just *stay*. Stick to the course.

This passage is a wonderful illustration of each concept above:

"Arise, my love, my beautiful one, and come away, for behold, the winter is past; the rain is over and gone. The flowers appear on the earth, the time of singing has come," (Song of Solomon 2:10-12a)

DISCUSSION QUESTIONS

Are praying, playing, and staying consistent themes in your relationship? Which of the three themes can you can improve in most?

What is one way you can grow in *each* area (praying, playing, staying)? Think of concrete examples.

HIS PRAYER

HER PRAYER

INTIMACY BEGINS
LONG BEFORE YOU
ENTER THE BEDROOM

DAY 21: THE THREE PROXIMITIES OF INTIMACY

Intimacy builds with every interaction. It happens with each glance, small touch, kind word, and inside joke you quietly laugh about when you're around others. If you're only intimate before and during sex, you're missing out. There's so much more! Intimacy is extreme closeness, and closeness can only happens with proximity. Consider these three areas of proximity:

1) Spiritual proximity. Are you both pursuing Jesus as your ultimate prize? Are you working out the meaning of the gospel daily, or does your 'relationship' with Jesus start and end with Sunday morning church? Journey *together* toward Christ.

2) Emotional proximity. Put in the time; discuss meaningful things. Ask open ended questions and leave room for lengthy answers. Try to understand how your spouse is feeling. Learn to empathize.

3) Physical proximity. If you're too busy to be around each other often, a lifestyle change is due. Work, hobbies, and general busyness will rob you of precious quality time. Then, when you're together, touch. Thoughtful, sincere touching will build a sweet sense of security and closeness.

Intimacy starts **long** before the bedroom by building closeness through purposeful proximity. It's helpful to remember that you belong to each other, so give of yourselves freely through proximity.

"For the wife does not have authority over her own body, but the husband does. Likewise the husband does not have authority over his own body, but the wife does." (1 Corinthians 7:4)

DISCUSSION QUESTIONS

What's one tangible way you can increase your closeness (proximity) in each area discussed?

<u>Spiritual proximity</u>

<u>Emotional proximity</u>

<u>Physical proximity</u>

HIS PRAYER

HER PRAYER

WHAT DRAWS PEOPLE TO BE FRIENDS
IS THAT THEY SEE THE SAME TRUTH;
THEY SHARE IT.

C.S. Lewis

DAY 22: SEEING THE SAME TRUTH

If we could give every couple we meet one piece of advice for marriage, it would be this: place your faith in Jesus, seek him first, and trust him together. He is the absolute best to be gained in life.

That's why this quote by C. S. Lewis is so relevant to marriage. Relationships start with friendship, and friends are drawn to one another by the same truth. But what is your "same truth"?

For many, this "same truth" is a common interest, hobby, or way of seeing the world. Jesus, however, is so much more than just an idea or hobby. When we see Jesus, we see truth *himself*. We see an entirely new reality with transformed hearts and a renewed vision of things. It is the pure truth of Jesus that gives godly marriage its strength. Without Christ being woven into every aspect of your relationship, you're easily broken. With him, you're unbreakable. Consider this timeless verse from Ecclesiastes:

"And though a man might prevail against one who is alone, two will withstand him—a threefold cord is not quickly broken." (Ecclesiastes 4:12)

If Lewis is right and friends are in fact drawn together by the same truth, then Jesus is the ultimate truth to attain and the most potent source of all you could hope for in your marriage. **See Jesus together.** Let him be the truth you share and the thread at the center of your threefold cord... never to be unwound, unravelled, or broken.

DISCUSSION QUESTIONS

What drew you to each other when you first met? What same truth(s) did you see then, and which do you see now?

How can you increase your unified vision of Jesus on a daily basis?

HIS PRAYER

HER PRAYER

HEALTHY MARRIAGE IS MUCH
MORE ABOUT CHRIST'S PERFECTION,
AND FAR LESS ABOUT YOUR OWN.

DAY 23: THIS GRACE IN WHICH WE STAND

"Through him we have also obtained access by faith into this grace in which we stand, and we rejoice in hope of the glory of God. Not only that, but we rejoice in our sufferings, knowing that suffering produces endurance, and endurance produces character, and character produces hope, and hope does not put us to shame," (Romans 5:2-5a)

It's astounding how much we are given in Christ and how little we do to earn it (nothing, in fact). We have access to God *himself*–a holy, powerful, perfect God–by faith alone, through "this grace which we stand". Before Jesus, a whiff of God's presence killed even the most righteous of men. But in Christ, **we stand**, by grace, through faith. The passage also says "we rejoice in sufferings". Wait...*what?*

It's peculiar that we can experience God's radical grace, stand in it, and rejoice. But it's even more bizarre that we **also** rejoice (*on the same level*) in our sufferings. Only Christ is big enough to allow this type of ridiculous rejoicing in all aspects of life, during every circumstance–good and bad.

That's why marriage is far more about Christ's perfection than your own. His perfect life, nailed to the cross, granted radical grace and reason to rejoice for all who believe. It's not *"fake it 'till you make it"*, it's realizing that in Christ, you have already "made it". This one truth changes how you approach your spouse. Your entire context shifts as you rest in Christ's work, not your own. In him you can act from a place of joy and security that empowers the type of selfless love your marriage always needs.

DISCUSSION QUESTIONS

What's more important for your marriage, your perfection or Christ's? Why?

At the beginning of the included passage, Paul mentions "this grace in which we stand". What does it mean to stand "in" grace?

HIS PRAYER

HER PRAYER

OUR FEELINGS OF LOVE
MAY COME AND GO,
BUT CHOOSING LOVE
IN ALL OCCASIONS IS
LOVE IN ITS TRUEST FORM

DAY 24: LOVE FOR ALL OCCASIONS

Love isn't always easy, but it's always worth it. That is precisely why marriage is designed to be a covenant relationship: the promise to love endures when the feelings of love are clouded.

The idea of covenant is one born in the mind of God, it's not a human concept. We see God show his covenental love throughout the Bible when he kept his promises though his people (us) didn't.

Jesus is the crescendo of God's covenantal commitment to us! He offered the greatest proof of his love for you on the cross. Not only that, he did it even though you don't deserve it in the least.

"...but God shows his love for us in that while we were still sinners, Christ died for us." (Romans 5:8)

While we were still sinners, Christ died. **Still**. Even in our sin–*despite our sin*–God loves us.

As you journey through marriage, remember that God knows what it's like to keep a covenant when it isn't easy. He wants to show you that brand of love and he longs for you to understand it. Your marriage is one of the most potent ways He does just that.

The next time feelings of love are sparse, remember that love is an action to be chosen. And by making the choice to love, you're honoring your covenant in deeply profound ways.

DISCUSSION QUESTIONS

When have you had to show love even though you didn't feel it?

Why did God design marriage as a covenant? How can marriage make the gospel more tangible in your life?

HIS PRAYER

HER PRAYER

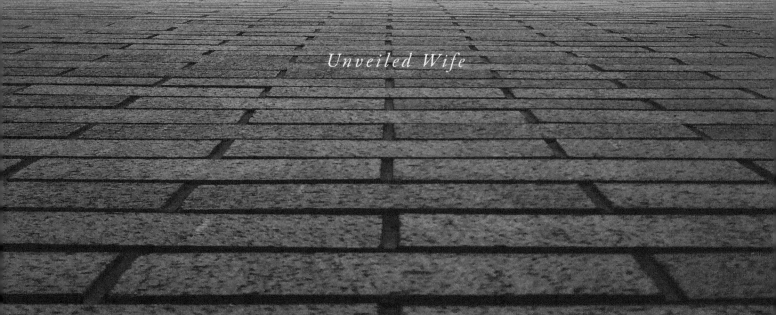

MARRIAGE IS A MOSAIC
YOU BUILD WITH YOUR SPOUSE,
MILLIONS OF TINY MOMENTS
THAT CREATE YOUR
LOVE STORY

Unveiled Wife

DAY 25: BEAUTIFUL IN-BETWEEN

One of the loveliest things about marriage is the plethora of "in-between" moments you share. It's in these tiny moments where you build your lives together, compiling your mosaic piece by piece.

The internet is filled with idealized images that are often planned, staged, rehearsed, shot, and tweaked to look just right so they convey a perfect moment in time. But have you ever wondered what's just outside the frame? What sort of reality extends beyond the edges of each photo, and what's happening *behind* the camera? If we could take a look, we'd most certainly see a reality that differs from the ideal. As a couple, you'll spend most of your marriage outside the frame. You experience *true* reality with one another–gritty, raw, and unrehearsed.

It's tempting to pursue life's best moments and discount the "in-between". We want to hop from mountain top to mountain top because summits are exhilarating and the view is incredible. However, trees don't grow on mountain tops! All growth happens in the valleys; real life exists between peaks.

Learn to treasure each small memory you share together–the good, the mediocre, and the bad. If you do, you'll better appreciate the vast majority of real life and more fully enjoy every tiny moment.

"Enjoy life with the wife whom you love, all the days of your vain life that he has given you under the sun, because that is your portion in life..." (Ecclesiastes 9:9a)

DISCUSSION QUESTIONS

In the image and quote, Jennifer Smith mentions "tiny moments". What are some of your favorite tiny moments together?

What does your average day look like? How can you better appreciate the "in-between" times?

108

HIS PRAYER

HER PRAYER

QUALITY TIME

RARELY HAPPENS

BY MISTAKE

DAY 26: DESIGN YOUR TIME

True quality time is becoming a lost art. There are more opportunities for wasting time than at any other period in history: smart phones, social media, streaming entertainment, 100s of cable channels, you name it. Paul urges us to use our time wisely:

"Look carefully then how you walk, not as unwise but as wise, making the best use of the time, because the days are evil. Therefore do not be foolish, but understand what the will of the Lord is."
(Ephesians 5:15-17)

If you don't give your attention to each other intentionally, there are many others who would like to steal it from you. Here are four ways to eliminate distraction and "design your time":

1) Schedule distraction free time. This could mean a weekly date, or a standing rule in your home where phones/screens go off at a certain time. Set parameters and stick to them.

2) Share a table once a day. Eat meals together whenever possible while sitting around your table. It sounds obvious, but only a small minority of families share a table daily.

3) Get comfortable with silence. Silence makes us uneasy. Try to fight that. Sometimes the best moments involve sitting, thinking, and filling the silence with genuine conversation.

4) Get outside as much as possible. God has given us a beautiful and vast planet. Get outside and breathe some fresh air! Walk, jog, eat, sit, talk... whatever your thing is, experience it outside together.

DISCUSSION QUESTIONS

Do you struggle with letting distractions steal your quality time? Why or why not?

What is **one** activity you can add to your routine that will consistently provide opportunities for quality time? Describe an ideal instance of that activity below.

HIS PRAYER

HER PRAYER

WORRYING CHANGES NOTHING

BUT FAITH IN JESUS

CHANGES EVERYTHING.

DAY 27: EXCHANGE FEAR FOR FAITH

We humans have a propensity for worry. We can get anxious about everything; even things we have zero power to control. Did you know that worrying is a subtle form of idolatry? When you worry about things in a way that steals your joy, you're believing that your situation or people in it have more power than God—that God won't care for you like he promises he will. Jesus spoke directly against this type of anxiety:

"Therefore I tell you, do not be anxious about your life, what you will eat or what you will drink, nor about your body, what you will put on. Is not life more than food, and the body more than clothing? Look at the birds of the air: they neither sow nor reap nor gather into barns, and yet your heavenly Father feeds them. Are you not of more value than they? And which of you by being anxious can add a single hour to his span of life?" (Matthew 6:25-27)

In marriage, there's plenty you can't control: each other's actions, your job, your children, their choices, and countless others. Every time anxiousness steals your joy, you set aside Christ's promises and erect false "fear idols". In those times, it's vital to remind yourself of God's promises.

There is freedom in truly believing in God's sovereignty! Take hold of his promises; always remind yourself of them when worry creeps in. Here's three promises to keep handy: God will care for you (Matt 6:30), stay with you (Heb 13:5), and work out every situation for good (Rom 8:28).

DISCUSSION QUESTIONS

What are a few areas you often worry about? What's the root of your anxiety?

Look up and write down at least two verses about God's promises that relate to your worries.

Explain how you can better rest in each promise in the future.

HIS PRAYER

HER PRAYER

LUST WOULD TAKE THE BODY
AND DISCARD THE SOUL.

LOVE DEEPLY DESIRES THE SOUL
AND GLADLY RECEIVES WHATEVER
BODY ACCOMPANIES IT.

DAY 28: LOVE VS LUST

It's important to make a sharp distinction between love and lust in marriage. When a husband and wife love each other's souls, time and aging only strengthen their love. Lust has the opposite effect. Understanding the differences between the two will help you address toxic tendencies directly.

Lust is selfish, love is selfless. Lust is shortsighted, love works with eternity in view. Lust is foolish, love is wise. Lust rushes, love is patient. Lust sees a person as an object to be used, love treats a person as a soul to be cherished.

Love is not bound by physical form or time. Love sees the soul and desires it, taking whatever body accompanies it. When you view each other through eyes of love, you see as God sees. Your attraction is as sure as the God in whose image you're made. This enduring attraction is vital for ensuring that your marriage continues to be the only arena for sexual expression and satisfaction.

"Drink water from your own cistern, flowing water from your own well. Should your springs be scattered abroad, streams of water in the streets? Let them be for yourself alone, and not for strangers with you." (Proverbs 5:15-17)

Lust corrupts your marriage but love vigilantly guards its purity. Determine to love! By choosing love over lust you're choosing God's way, which always leads to life.

DISCUSSION QUESTIONS

What does it mean to "love your spouse's soul"?

In your own words, what is the biggest difference between love and lust?

HIS PRAYER

HER PRAYER

MODELING A HEALTHY MARRIAGE
IS ONE OF THE BEST GIFTS
YOU CAN GIVE YOUR CHILD.

Dr. Gary Chapman

DAY 29: A GENERATIONAL GIFT

God's design for marriage is also his design for family. Countless studies show the necessity and benefit of raising children in stable homes with one father and one mother who are both present and involved. When you fight for the health of your marriage, you fight for the health of your kids. Your family legacy starts today and echos for generations to come. (*Sound heavy enough?*)

That is precisely why marriage is designed to be a covenant relationship. It is the framework needed for stability and the anchor that holds fast amidst even the most tumultuous of storms. With so much at stake, the burden of perfection is absolutely crushing. What if your anchor fails? That's why we must hold fast to someone vastly bigger, more holy, and far stronger than we are in ourselves: Christ.

"For people swear by something greater than themselves, and in all their disputes an oath is final for confirmation. So when God desired to show more convincingly to the heirs of the promise the unchangeable character of his purpose, he guaranteed it with an oath... We have this as a sure and steadfast anchor of the soul, a hope that enters into the inner place behind the curtain, where Jesus has gone as a forerunner on our behalf" (Hebrews 6:16-17, 19-20a)

Attach yourselves to the anchor (Jesus) and stay in the ship (your marriage)! Then, rest secure through every storm knowing that your anchor is sure. Remember that your covenant is a framework designed by God himself for his glory, your health, and the benefit of generations to come.

DISCUSSION QUESTIONS

Do you have a "family vision statement"? Imagine your household 10 and 20 years from today. What do you see? Set aside an hour (now or in the near future) to discuss your family vision in detail.

Here's a start:

We envision a family that _____ *and a household that's* _____ .

HIS PRAYER

HER PRAYER

LOVE ENDURES ALL

DAY 30: LOVE ENDURES ALL THINGS

What does it mean in 1 Corinthians 13 where it says *"love endures all things"*? While the context of the Bible's classic love chapter is referring to spiritual giftings within the church, the characteristics of love are immensely relevant for marriage. Carefully consider each aspect of love below:

"Love is patient and kind; love does not envy or boast; it is not arrogant or rude. It does not insist on its own way; it is not irritable or resentful; it does not rejoice at wrongdoing, but rejoices with the truth. Love bears all things, believes all things, hopes all things, endures all things." (1 Corinthians 13:5-7)

"Love endures." The most potent aspect of love's endurance is patience. Being patient seems harder than ever since we live in an age of instant gratification. Regardless, love should endure.

Patience in marriage is the difference between peace and chaos, unity and bickering, joy and discord. You can show patience to each other in small ways by overlooking annoyances, and you can show it in larger ways by taking time to work through tougher issues.

Most of all, God's love endures as he works on your hearts. His enduring love always transforms. God isn't finished with either of you yet, so don't give up on each other! God won't.

Patience is where grace and time join paths. Be patient in big things and small, and in doing so, love.

DISCUSSION QUESTIONS

How can you love each other more patiently? Cite a few real examples.

How would having more patience impact your marriage?

HIS PRAYER

HER PRAYER

BONUS IMAGES

We hope you've been refreshed and challenged by this devotional. It's important that you continue reminding yourselves to love each other intentionally. In the following pages, we've included **10 bonus images** to help you do just that!

We encourage you to **cut a few pages from this book.** Write a few reasons why it's important to you on the back of each image. Get creative with how and where you display them in your home or work space. Also feel free to clip a few images from the devotional pages; they were designed for that!

Here are some ideas for how to use images cut from this book:

- Hang several on a string (or wire) by attaching with mini spring clothespins

- Use Modge Podge to secure an image to a plank of wood (the back will be sealed in, but you can use it as a "time capsule" to be cut open along the edges and read at a future date!)

- Prop them up on a shelf or ledge; stack a few and rotate the top image every day, week, or month

- Mount one in a picture frame to hang on your wall

Get creative! However you use them, we hope they inspire and remind you to love your spouse well.

*NOTE: each left-side page is used for writing on the **back of the preceding image.***

WHEN I'VE LEARNT TO LOVE GOD
BETTER THAN MY EARTHLY DEAREST,
I'LL LOVE MY EARTHLY DEAREST
BETTER THAN I DO NOW.

C. S. Lewis

THIS IMAGE MATTERS TO US BECAUSE...

Why is this image (on the flipside) important to you?

TWO AS **ONE**
AN [INSTAVOTIONAL]™

TRUE LOVE

IS FRIENDSHIP

SET ON FIRE

THIS IMAGE MATTERS TO US BECAUSE...

Why is this image (on the flipside) important to you?

TWO AS **ONE**
AN [INSTAVOTIONAL]™

LOVE MEANS LOVING THE UNLOVABLE
OR IT IS NO VIRTUE AT ALL.

G. K. Chesterton

THIS IMAGE MATTERS TO US BECAUSE...

⤺ Why is this image (on the flipside) important to you?

TWO AS ONE
AN [INSTAVOTIONAL]™

LET ALL THAT YOU DO

BE DONE IN LOVE

1 Corinthians 16:14

THIS IMAGE MATTERS TO US BECAUSE...

Why is this image (on the flipside) important to you?

TWO AS **ONE**
AN [INSTAVOTIONAL]™

WHAT COUNTS IN MAKING A HAPPY
MARRIAGE IS NOT SO MUCH HOW
COMPATIBLE YOU ARE, BUT HOW
YOU DEAL WITH INCOMPATIBILITY

Leo Tolstoy

THIS IMAGE MATTERS TO US BECAUSE...

Why is this image (on the flipside) important to you?

TWO AS **ONE**
AN [INSTAVOTIONAL]™

A HAPPY MARRIAGE IS A LONG
CONVERSATION WHICH ALWAYS
SEEMS TOO SHORT.

André Maurois

THIS IMAGE MATTERS TO US BECAUSE...

Why is this image (on the flipside) important to you?

TWO AS **ONE**
AN [INSTAVOTIONAL]™

LOVE RELENTLESSLY

Why is this image (on the flipside) important to you?

TWO AS **ONE**
AN [INSTAVOTIONAL]

COVENANT LOVE SAYS
"I DO EVEN IF YOU DON'T"
&
"I WILL EVEN IF YOU WON'T"

THIS IMAGE MATTERS TO US BECAUSE...

Why is this image (on the flipside) important to you?

TWO AS **ONE**
AN [INSTAVOTIONAL]

LOVE IS A GRAND ADVENTURE
WHERE THE JOURNEY IS THE GOAL
AND THE DESTINATION IS EACH OTHER

THIS IMAGE MATTERS TO US BECAUSE...

Why is this image (on the flipside) important to you?

TWO AS ONE
AN [INSTAVOTIONAL]™

WE LOVE BECAUSE HE FIRST LOVED US

1 John 4:19

THIS IMAGE MATTERS TO US BECAUSE...

Why is this image (on the flipside) important to you?

TWO AS ONE
AN [INSTAVOTIONAL]™

ADDITIONAL RESOURCES

We're passionate about pointing couples to Christ and strengthening marriages. We write weekly on our blog and release new content daily via social media. Make sure to find us online!

- FierceMarriage.com *(our website)*

- FierceMarriage.com/List *(join our e-mail list to get articles & special updates in your inbox)*

- Facebook.com/FierceMarriage

- Instagram.com/FierceMarriage

- YouTube.com/FierceMarriage

- Twitter.com/FierceMarriage

RECOMMENDED BOOKS

For a list of books we love, please visit **FierceMarriage.com/Resources**

DO YOU HAVE FEEDBACK?

We'd love to hear from you. If you have any comments about this book, or if you'd like to share how it helped your marriage, please send an email to **feedback@fiercemarriage.com**

CARE TO LEAVE A REVIEW?

If you've enjoyed this book, **we'd be honored if you wrote a 5-star review** wherevever you purchased your copy (Amazon.com or otherwise)! Share a testimony of what God's doing in your marriage, and watch as your story ministers to others! You never know who might read it and be encouraged.

GROUP STUDY LEADERS

If you would like to lead a small group based on this devotional, bulk discounts are available (8+). Please email us with details at **groups@fiercemarriage.com** and we'll be in touch shortly!

SPEAKING REQUESTS

For all speaking inquiries, kindly send all details in an email to **speaking@fiercemarriage.com**.

Made in the USA
Columbia, SC
15 May 2017